OVERLAND STAGE

*The story of the famous Overland Stagecoaches
of the 1860's*

Mail Coach

OVERLAND STAGE

The story of the famous Overland Stagecoaches of the 1860's

Printed in the United States of America

Written and Illustrated by GLEN DINES

© Harry G. Dines 1961
Library of Congress catalog card number: 61-17257
First printing
The Macmillan Company, New York
Brett-Macmillan Ltd., Galt, Ontario

THE MACMILLAN COMPANY
New York
1961

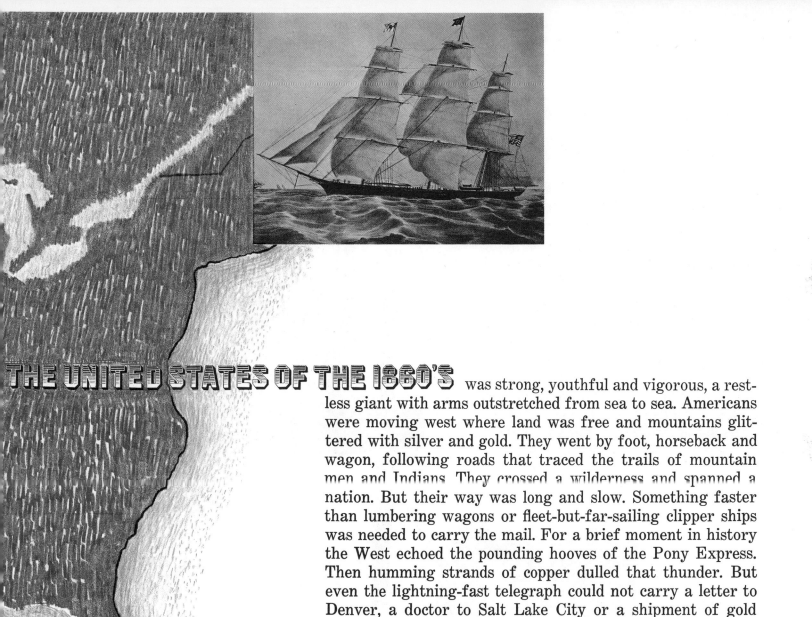

THE UNITED STATES OF THE 1860'S

was strong, youthful and vigorous, a restless giant with arms outstretched from sea to sea. Americans were moving west where land was free and mountains glittered with silver and gold. They went by foot, horseback and wagon, following roads that traced the trails of mountain men and Indians. They crossed a wilderness and spanned a nation. But their way was long and slow. Something faster than lumbering wagons or fleet-but-far-sailing clipper ships was needed to carry the mail. For a brief moment in history the West echoed the pounding hooves of the Pony Express. Then humming strands of copper dulled that thunder. But even the lightning-fast telegraph could not carry a letter to Denver, a doctor to Salt Lake City or a shipment of gold bullion to San Francisco. Wires alone could not link the arms of this giant.

From the east came the answer—born of New England skill and named after the New Hampshire town in which they were built—the famous Concord overland stagecoaches.

Big for the job, they weighed over a ton, stood 8 feet tall and left a track 5½ feet wide. Yet each coach was handmade of the finest wood. Each piece, from the tiniest cleat to one of the massive 7-foot perches, was fashioned and fitted and finished with patient craftsmanship. The graceful bass-wood panels were steamed and curved to fit stout ash frames. The planks were hewn of clearest pine and birch. The wheels, with hubs of specially seasoned elm, were rimmed with hardest hickory and spoked with tough oak. The best parts of 14 selected steer hides went into the boots and thorough braces. Where extra strength was needed, wood was strapped with iron and bolted through. Nearly every stagecoach that rumbled overland in the '60's was a ruggedly handsome Mail Coach or a lighter, canvas-topped "Mud Wagon," built by Abbot, Downing of Concord, New Hampshire.

A "Mud Wagon" from Abbot, Downing and Company, 1870 catalogue. Price—$625.00. The same catalogue lists a nine-passenger Mail Coach, complete, at $1120.

1—Rear boot, platform hinged to coach and supported by two chains, apron and sides of leather.

2—Driver's box and front boot, leather sides.

3—Candle lamp, one on each side.

4—Leather curtains, roll-down, damask-lined.

5—Panel opening, fitted with sliding glass window.

6—Door window, fitted with sliding glass window.

7—Metal reenforcement braces, three on each side.

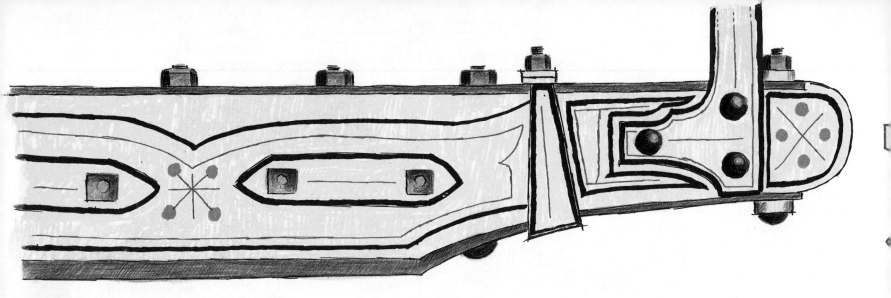

The overland coaches were painted as carefully as they were built. Bold, manly colors were used—vermilion, yellow, red and black. Their sides were decorated with handsome gilt scrolls. Colorful pictures were painted on each door, the work of skilled artists, these paintings were mostly landscapes with no two alike. Well known landmarks were also popular and sometimes there were portraits of famous people. The panels, wheels and ironwork were skillfully striped and even the unseen parts of the undercarriage were decorated.

The name of the company ordering the coach was usually lettered above the windows. U.S. Mail or U.S.M. often appeared at the tops of the doors. Sometimes a driver's name was lettered on the side of the box and the coach itself christened with a name like *Argosy, Western Monarch* or *Prairie Queen*. The entire coach was coated with tough, glass-smooth varnish after the decoration was completed.

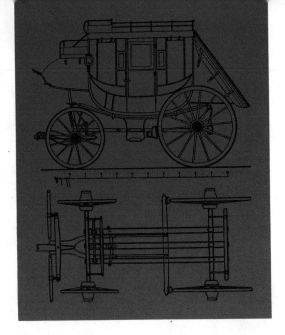

THOROUGHBRACE
STANDARD

But the Concords were not all glitter and gilt. They were also plain tough. An example was the famous "Deadwood Stage," shown throughout the world in Buffalo Bill Cody's Wild West Show. This Concord Mail Coach, built in 1868 and shipped to California by clipper, was first used in the Sierra Nevadas, then in the Rockies and finally on the route between Cheyenne, Wyoming and Deadwood in the jagged Black Hills of South Dakota. After some 27 years of rough mountain roads, the running gear of this battered old veteran was still in good order.

One of the reasons for this toughness was the thorough brace slings—the "springs" of the Concords. These many-layered leather "hammocks" gave a swinging forward and backward motion which helped both coach and team over the roughest of frontier roads.

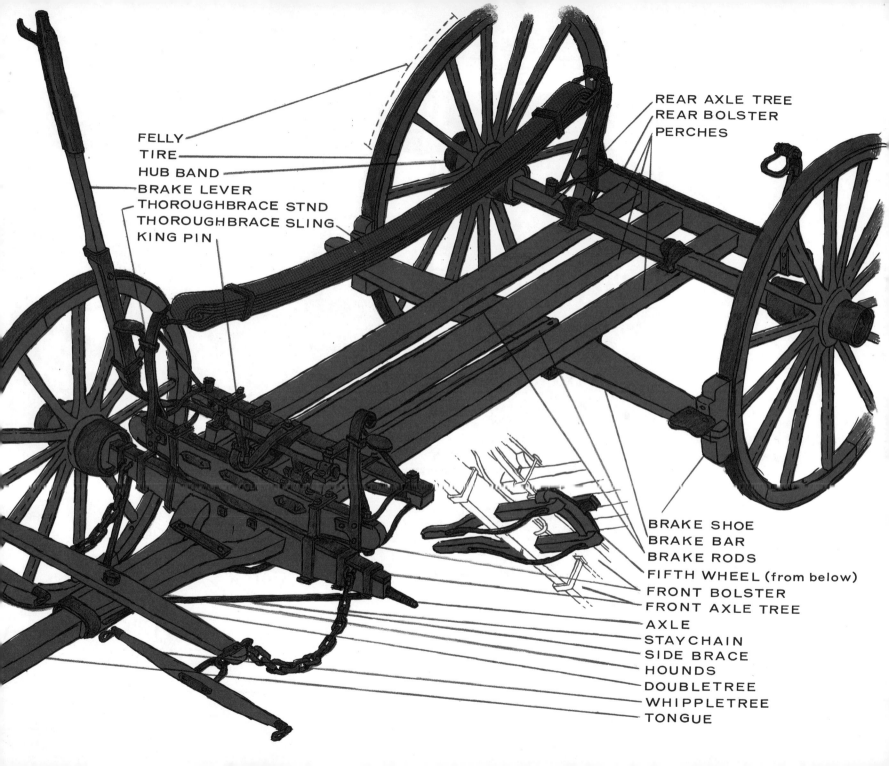

FELLY

TIRE

HUB BAND

BRAKE LEVER

THOROUGHBRACE STND

THOROUGHBRACE SLING

KING PIN

REAR AXLE TREE

REAR BOLSTER

PERCHES

BRAKE SHOE

BRAKE BAR

BRAKE RODS

FIFTH WHEEL (from below)

FRONT BOLSTER

FRONT AXLE TREE

AXLE

STAYCHAIN

SIDE BRACE

HOUNDS

DOUBLETREE

WHIPPLETREE

TONGUE

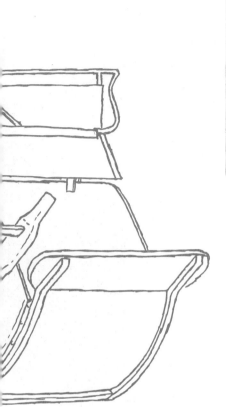

On the frontier, where a common kitchen chair was often a rarity, the leather-covered, well padded seats of a Mail Coach were sheer luxury. A standard nine-passenger coach had two high-backed seats facing each other and a "jump" seat (1) with a wide, leather band (2) as back rest. Both ends of this narrow bench folded up and inward. Topside, many of the coaches were equipped to seat 8 more passengers; three in the "dickey" seat (3), three in the deck seat (4) and two squeezed beside the driver in the messenger's seat (5). Sometimes passengers even slept on the top deck, after spreading hay and blankets and tying themselves securely.

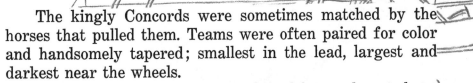

The kingly Concords were sometimes matched by the horses that pulled them. Teams were often paired for color and handsomely tapered; smallest in the lead, largest and darkest near the wheels.

Stage horses, however, were selected for work, not show. Sorrels, bays, brindles, grays, they varied from gamy western stock to big 1500-pound Kentucky-bred trotters.

New horses were usually carefully trained, making their first runs beside veterans who knew their jobs and the road almost as well as the driver. With good care they worked their 10 to 20 miles day after day, year after year. A sorrel in California made his run every day for 15 years—nearly a quarter million miles! And, possibly, he did his work in a harness of J. R. Hill and Company of Concord or Main and Winchester of San Francisco, famous makers of rugged, lightweight, "fast hitch" stage harness.

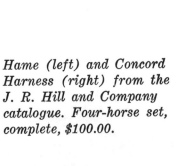

**Common Hame.
No. 12.**

Hame (left) and Concord Harness (right) from the J. R. Hill and Company catalogue. Four-horse set, complete, $100.00.

1. *Crupper*
2. *Lines*
3. *Breeching*
4. *Breast strap*
5. *Spreader*
6. *Toggle*
7. *Trace*

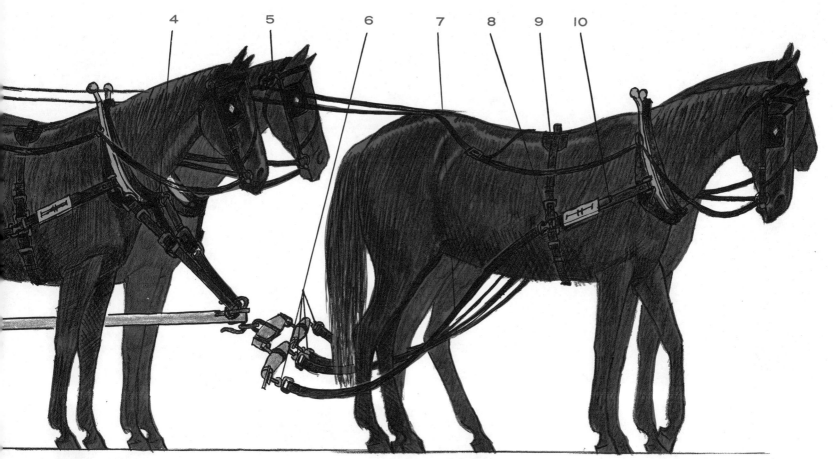

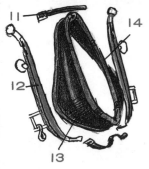

11
14
12
13

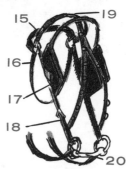

15   19
16
17
18   20

8. Belly band
9. Back band and pad
10. Hame tug
11. Hame strap
12. Hame
13. Collar
14. Collar pad

Parts of Bridle
15. Crown
16. Throat strap
17. Blind
18. Cheek strap
19. Brow band
20. Bit

Newspaper advertisement of the mid '60's, from the famous "Rocky Mountain News" of Denver, Colorado.

Tuesday, 7:52 A.M., sometime in the mid-1860's. Shimmering in the Kansas sun, a scarlet red Concord stands before the Overland Stage depot in Atchison. Departure time in eight minutes. As the last of the luggage is loaded into the rear boot, a late arriving passenger scurries across the dusty street. He might be a young mining engineer, a salesman or a lawyer. Whatever his work, his name is on the passenger list, destination Placerville, and he has paid the $325.00 fare in full.

Because of the 25-pound limit on luggage, he is wearing an extra pair of trousers and shirt. For small comfort and safety, the pockets of his overcoat are stuffed with socks, a woolen scarf, several cans of sardines, some hardtack, a water bottle, a bar of soap, toilet articles and 20 rounds of ammunition for his Sharps carbine.

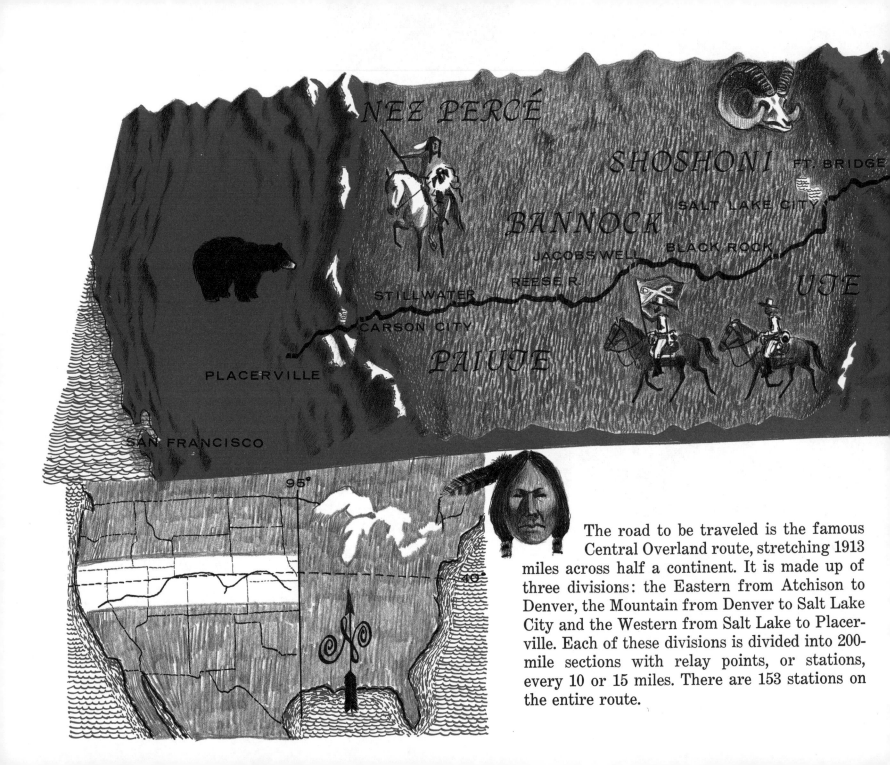

NEZ PERCÉ

SHOSHONI

FT. BRIDGE

SALT LAKE CITY

BANNOCK

JACOBS WELL

BLACK ROCK

REESE R.

STILLWATER

UTE

CARSON CITY

PAIUTE

PLACERVILLE

SAN FRANCISCO

95°

40°

The road to be traveled is the famous Central Overland route, stretching 1913 miles across half a continent. It is made up of three divisions: the Eastern from Atchison to Denver, the Mountain from Denver to Salt Lake City and the Western from Salt Lake to Placerville. Each of these divisions is divided into 200-mile sections with relay points, or stations, every 10 or 15 miles. There are 153 stations on the entire route.

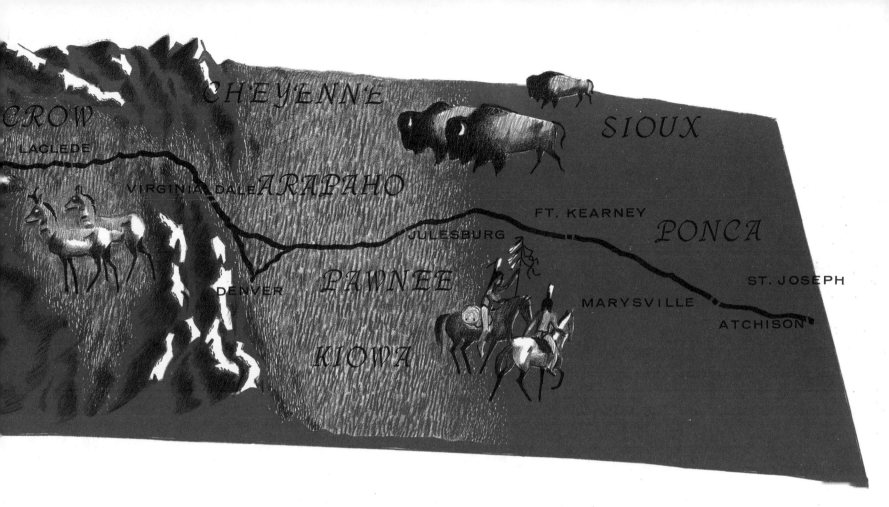

It is a mountain road for the most part, spanning the massive Rockies, the Wasatch, the riblike ranges of the Great Basin and the granite-capped Sierra Nevadas of California. For more than 1300 miles it never dips lower than one mile above sea level as it winds through the breeding grounds of blizzards, cloudbursts, scourging sandstorms and the fickle mountain creeks that can change into raging rivers overnight.

Yet storms pass and a stream can be bridged, but the swift and deadly Plains Indians, like the Sioux and Cheyenne, the Arapaho and Ute, must be either outfought or outrun. And the Overland road cuts through the very heartland of these warrior tribes.

Still, there is a schedule to make, and at exactly 8:00 o'clock the big red Concord rolls out across the Kansas prairie bound for Placerville, 19 days away—with luck.

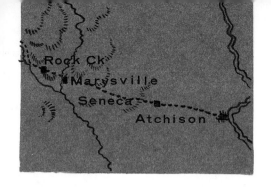

The road is dry and there's a nip in the morning air. Between stations the teams are "let out." Flashing into Lancaster, Kennekuk and Kickapoo, the lurching Concord fills the prairie with the thunder of hooves, the pop and snap of harness, the jangly clink of brass and steel. From above come the shouts of the driver. "Hi-yi! G'lang! Up thar, Dutch! Go you, Red!"

A passenger riding beside the driver clutches the railing. Inside the drumming coach, trunks and mail sacks toss and tumble to the throb of the thudding wheels.

Ft. Kearny

Pawnee

Kiowa

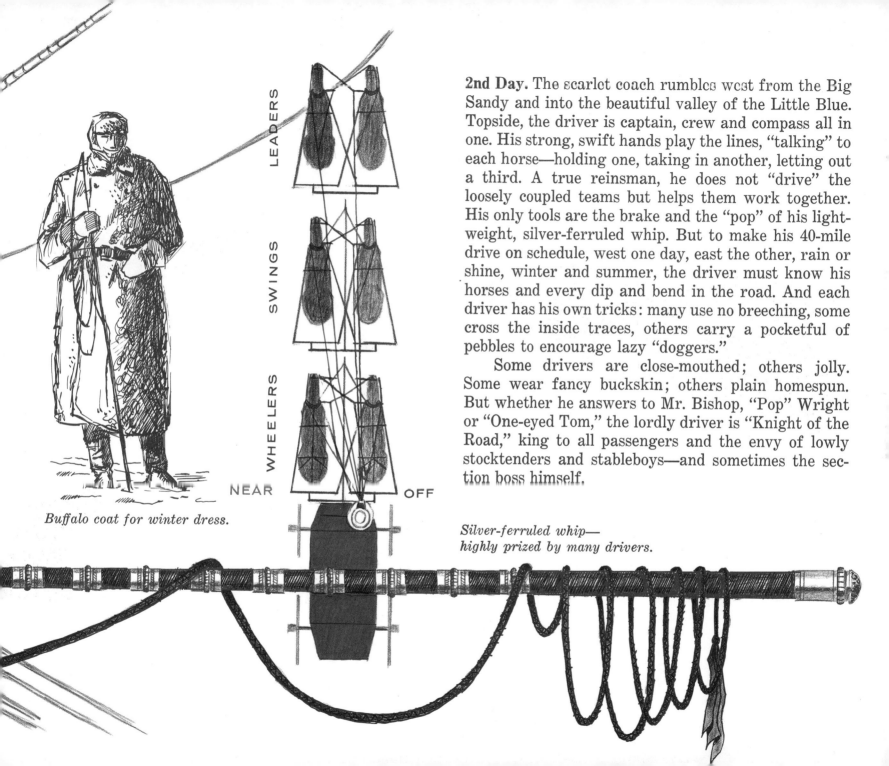

LEADERS

SWINGS

WHEELERS

NEAR   OFF

Buffalo coat for winter dress.

*Silver-ferruled whip—
highly prized by many drivers.*

2nd Day. The scarlet coach rumbles west from the Big Sandy and into the beautiful valley of the Little Blue. Topside, the driver is captain, crew and compass all in one. His strong, swift hands play the lines, "talking" to each horse—holding one, taking in another, letting out a third. A true reinsman, he does not "drive" the loosely coupled teams but helps them work together. His only tools are the brake and the "pop" of his lightweight, silver-ferruled whip. But to make his 40-mile drive on schedule, west one day, east the other, rain or shine, winter and summer, the driver must know his horses and every dip and bend in the road. And each driver has his own tricks: many use no breeching, some cross the inside traces, others carry a pocketful of pebbles to encourage lazy "doggers."

Some drivers are close-mouthed; others jolly. Some wear fancy buckskin; others plain homespun. But whether he answers to Mr. Bishop, "Pop" Wright or "One-eyed Tom," the lordly driver is "Knight of the Road," king to all passengers and the envy of lowly stocktenders and stableboys—and sometimes the section boss himself.

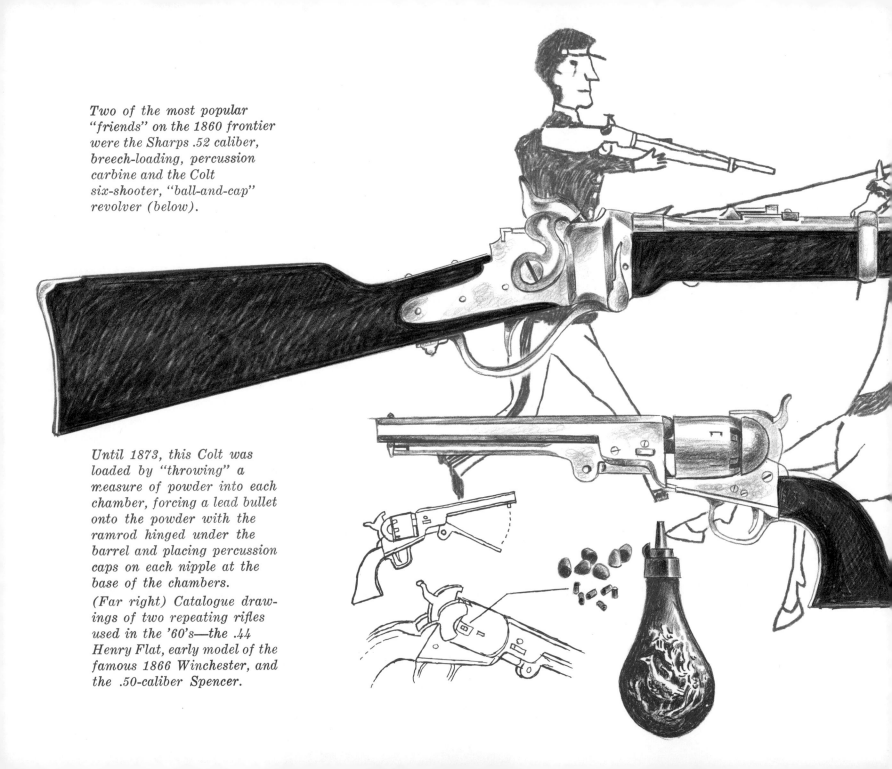

Two of the most popular "friends" on the 1860 frontier were the Sharps .52 caliber, breech-loading, percussion carbine and the Colt six-shooter, "ball-and-cap" revolver (below).

Until 1873, this Colt was loaded by "throwing" a measure of powder into each chamber, forcing a lead bullet onto the powder with the ramrod hinged under the barrel and placing percussion caps on each nipple at the base of the chambers.

(Far right) Catalogue drawings of two repeating rifles used in the '60's—the .44 Henry Flat, early model of the famous 1866 Winchester, and the .50-caliber Spencer.

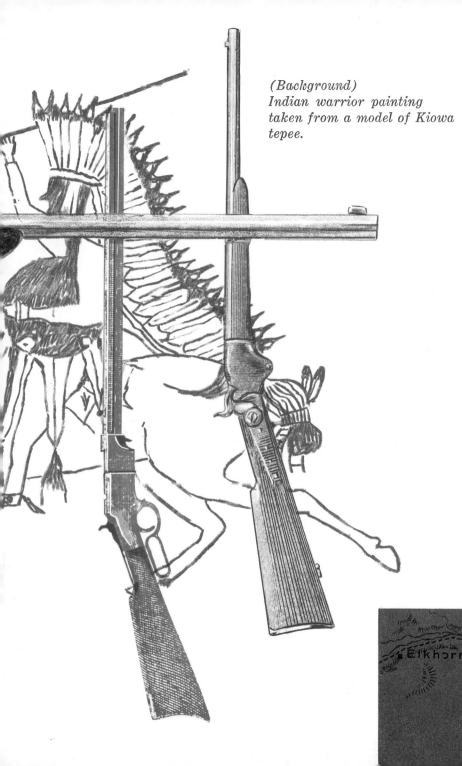

(Background)
Indian warrior painting taken from a model of Kiowa tepee.

3rd Day. Skirting the south bank of the broad and twisting Platte River, the stage flashes past a long train of lumbering freight wagons. The air is thick with dust. The "bullwhackers'" whips crack like pistol shots. West from Ft. Kearny it's uphill all the way to Denver, 400 miles of water grade. Some of the finest stock is strung along this division—horses, as well as the big five-mule "spike" teams that pull the stage through the worst stretches of heavy sand.

West of Ft. Kearny the gently rolling prairie gives way to sand hills, twisting gullies and the thin, clumpy grass of the high plains. For miles at a stretch the roadside is pocked with the rimmed holes of yip-yapping prairie dogs. The stage rocks across ancient buffalo trails cut in the valley floor. A few shaggy forms are spotted on the rim of a distant bluff but the driver can remember when great herds sometimes blocked the road.

A column of U.S. Cavalry jogs into view, men and horses streaked with sweat. Two saddles are empty. Both driver and passengers look to their guns as the road ahead curves out of sight among steep sand bluffs.

West of Ft. Kearny the frontier begins.

Plains Indian shield.

The driver spots them first—three young braves on horseback standing in the road ahead. They motion him to stop. He answers with a quick snap of the whip. The team breaks into a gallop. Arrows buzz angrily as the Indians charge forward, then swerve. More arrows hiss to the crack of pistols.

"War party!" someone shouts.

The driver shakes his head. "Not this time. These lads are jist playin' Injin tag." Nevertheless he keeps the team at a smart pace as they pound across the flat, sage plains that boarder the South Platte.

In many areas the countryside was covered with the sun-bleeched bones of buffalo, killed for their hides alone and left to be picked clean by animals and birds.

But many "swing" station stock tenders are wanted by the law and glad to exchange the rugged, dangerous life of an isolated stage station for that of a prison cell. To this rough, scraggly-bearded crew a Saturday night "bath" means draping blankets and underwear across a nearby ant hill so that the ants can feast on the lice and bedbugs.

"Leastwise," they explain, "you can see an ant."

7th Day. The passengers are strangely silent as the stage rocks north out of Denver. There are reports of Indian trouble along the line—not like last year when stations and ranches on whole sections were attacked and burned or abandoned—but bad enough with several stations attacked, horses stolen and a stock tender killed.

The driver reins in before a lonely "swing" station and glances nervously about as the fresh team is hitched. Tiny, one-room cabins like these, with two or three men to guard a dozen or more horses, are favorite targets for raiding Indians.

Hand-operated coffee grinder.

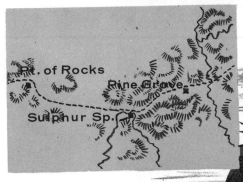

8th Day. At high noon a cluster of stone and log buildings comes as a welcome sight. It is the end of this driver's run and a famous stopping place because his wife is one of the best cooks west of Denver. Almost before the stage stops rolling, the passengers are crowding into the small kitchen-dining room of the sod-roofed station house.

After a delicious dinner of antelope steaks, freshly baked bread, pickles, apple pie and ever-present coffee —well worth the $2.00 price—several passengers hurry down to the nearby creek for a quick "bath," despite the pesky "buffalo flies" and mosquitoes. Others wander about the well kept ranch that includes a hayfield, a barn, several sheds and a blacksmith and carriage repair shop. The station house boasts two "overnight" sleeping rooms with real feather beds. A far cry from the bigger home stations on the route, but better than most.

Meanwhile a new coach is brought up and its axles greased. After the luggage and mail sacks are transferred and a fresh team is hitched, the passengers and new driver climb aboard and the stage rocks westward once again. It lurches through huge, trenchlike Bridger Pass and out into the butte-studded Bitter Creek country.

Right—On the Express or Messenger coaches which regularly carried valuable freight, the treasure box was sometimes "built in" beneath the rear seat.

Above—Double-barreled, muzzle-loaded, "sawed-off" shotgun—deadly at short range and the favorite of many stagecoach messengers in the '60's.

9th Day. In the bleak sage desert west of Green River, the "Cherokee Trail" short cut—begun some 300 miles to the east—comes to an end. The stage swings south along the Black Fork to bump and sway once again in the ruts of the famous old Oregon Trail. And, once again, the poles of the transcontinental telegraph flick past the coach windows.

Old Fort Bridger, an oasis of cottonwood and willow, is cluttered with the wagons of a huge eastbound freight train. To the south the jagged peaks of the Unita Mountains loom darkly against a predawn sky.

Just before the stage pulls out, an iron-bound treasure box is hoisted into the front boot and a company messenger swings up beside the driver. Stagecoach robberies are common on the branch lines to the north and in ore-rich Nevada and California and there are reports of some buffalo-hunters-turned-outlaw lurking in the hills near Muddy Creek. However, the veteran driver is not too worried.

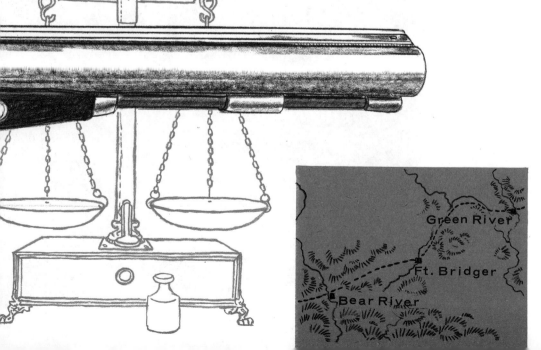

Short-barreled "Wells Fargo" Colt revolver—used in the 1870's.

A "one candle power"
stagecoach lamp.

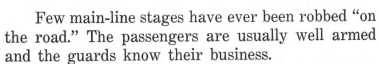

Few main-line stages have ever been robbed "on the road." The passengers are usually well armed and the guards know their business.

On the morning of the tenth day the stage thunders into red-rimmed Echo Canyon, pathway through the Wasatch for the Mormon pioneers and many California-bound emigrants. In lush Weber River Valley the route hooks south past Kimball's Junction on the westernmost section of Ben Holladay's Overland Stage Line. In neat, bustling Salt Lake City the "through" passengers board a Concord of the Overland Mail Company and grate westward across an ancient, salt-crusted lake bed. Handling the lines is an old-timer who drove a Celerity Wagon on the Southern Overland route. This was the famous Butterfield Line that carried the mail from St. Louis through El Paso and into southern California until the outbreak of the Civil War.

Ruby Valley

Deer Ck.

Roberts Ck.

Schell Ck.

13th Day. Hour after hour the stage grinds across a gigantic washboard of sage flats and scrub-stubbled mountain ranges. In the basins the wheels cut deeply, churning up itchy alkali grit that cakes on driver, passengers and sweat-lathered horses alike. In the mountains the burn of dust gives way to spine-jarring thuds as the stage pounds and plunges through narrow rock-strewn passes.

It is a big land—harsh and unyielding—yet vastly beautiful.

On the sixteenth day the stage carries a special passenger—the Division Superintendent himself—once a driver, now chief of a small army of section bosses, clerks, bookkeepers, drivers, blacksmiths, harness makers, farriers, carpenters, wainwrights, stationmasters and stock tenders who keep the coaches rolling.

Also in his charge are twenty to thirty teamsters, whose lumbering freight wagons supply the stations. For the more than 550 horses on this division alone, some seven tons of feed are needed every day—nearly three thousand tons a year. And at a few stations every buckle, bean and drop of water must be hauled in by wagon.

Choking in the dust of a "washoe" blowing down from the Sierras, the driver reins up in "rip-roarin'," silver-rich Carson City on the afternoon of the seventeenth day.

A stage of the Pioneer Line carries the passengers and mail south to Genoa, then west through rugged Daggett Pass and into California.

Here, in California, western staging was born. Hard on the heels of the first gold strike in '49, stagecoaches began rolling regularly through the Mother Lode country. By 1853, when much of the mail carried west from the Mississippi went by mule wagon, handsome Concords, brought " 'round the horn" in Clippers, were rumbling over the 1500-mile route of the California Stage Company. In 1857, when Denver was just starting to grow, a Concord of the famous Pioneer Stage Company made the first stagecoach crossing over the towering Sierras.

It is fitting that a coach of this proud line—to many the best west of the Missouri—should tick off the last few miles of the overland route. It skirts the south tip of Lake Tahoe, struggles over 7000-foot Echo Summit, thunders down the narrow canyon of the South Fork of the American River and stops at last, on the nineteenth day, before the ornate Cary House in Placerville.

CALIFORNIA
STAGE COMPANY.

RUN DAILY LINES OF COACHES
FROM
SACRAMENTO,
Communicating with all the
INTERIOR TOWNS AND MINES.

OFFICE OF THE COMPANY,
ORLEANS HOTEL
JAMES HA__TH

G. J. WOODY Nº 2

PIONEER
STAGE LINE
USM & WF EXP

*In the '50's there were often a dozen stages leaving
Sacramento each day, bound for places like Angel's Camp,
Yankee Jim's, Murderer's Bar, Dry Town, Rough and Ready
or Secret Diggin's.*

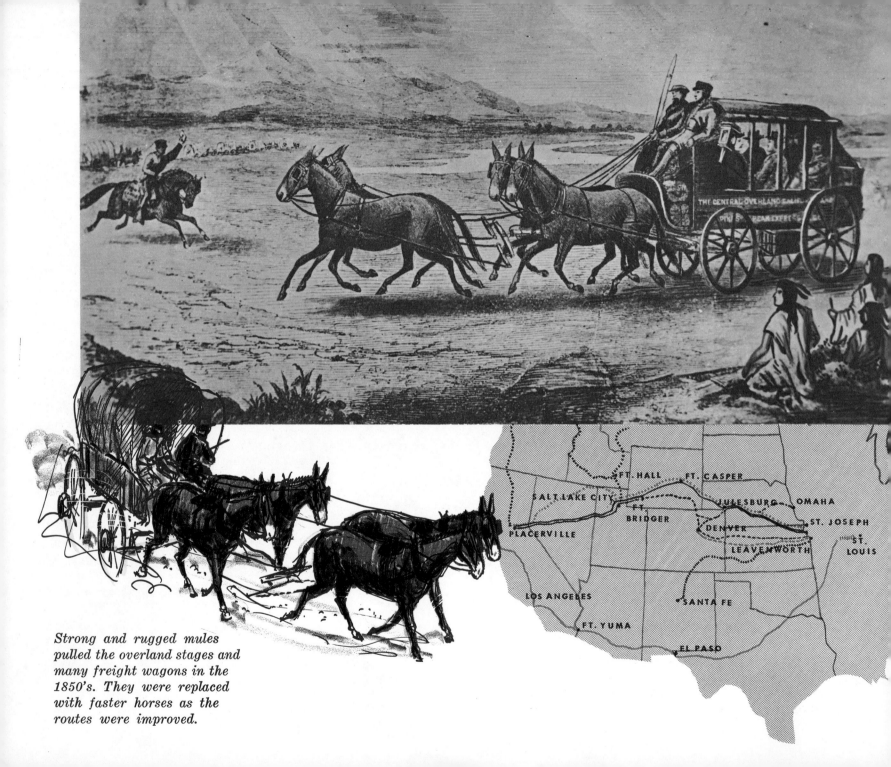

Strong and rugged mules
pulled the overland stages and
many freight wagons in the
1850's. They were replaced
with faster horses as the
routes were improved.

FT. HALL FT. CASPER

SALT LAKE CITY

FT.
BRIDGER

JULESBURG OMAHA

ST. JOSEPH

DENVER

PLACERVILLE

LEAVENWORTH

ST.
LOUIS

LOS ANGELES

SANTA FE

FT. YUMA

EL PASO

Central Overland (Chorpenning/Hockaday)
Leavenworth and Pike's Peak Express
C.O.C. and P.P.E.
"Cherokee Trail" cutoff
Great Southern Overland Mail route
Santa Fe Mail
(David) Butterfield Overland Despatch
Western Stage Company

Out of the California Overland Mail Act of 1857 and Chorpenning and Hockaday's struggling Central Overland came the Central Overland California and Pike's Peak Express, under the ownership of Russell, Majors and Waddell. This giant freighting concern also owned the fabulous Pony Express. When the ponies folded in 1861 so did their owners, and the C.O.C. and P.P.E. became Benjamin Holladay's Overland Stage Company. In the mid-'60's the overland route was the backbone of a 3000-mile stagecoach empire, which included the Western Stage Company, the Butterfield Overland Despatch, and the branch lines to Oregon, Idaho and Montana.

Late in 1866, famous Wells-Fargo and Company bought out Holladay, but the overland route was fast shrinking. In May, 1869, the transcontinental railroad was completed and the wheels of hickory that had bridged a nation gave way to stronger and faster wheels of steel.

GLOSSARY

Definitions of special words and terms which are not fully explained in text and pictures.

boot. Storage compartment.

"bullwhacker." Driver of oxen-pulled freight wagon.

damask. Heavy, figured fabric of linen, silk, wool, etc.

division. Portion of route made up of a number of drives.

Division Supervisor. One in charge of a division; division agent.

drive. Portion of route between home stations.

Express coach. Regularly scheduled coach carrying valuable freight; Messenger coach.

Express messenger. Guard for valuable freight; employee of stage line or separate express company; "shotgun rider."

farrier. Blacksmith, especially one who shoes horses.

General Supervisor. One in charge of entire stagecoach line.

hand. 4 inches, as a horse is 15 hands or 5 feet tall.

home station. Relay point along route where teams are changed and meal served to passengers, usually home of driver.

lead team. Foremost team.

mule. Offspring of male ass and mare.

near. Left side.

off. Right side.

pole. Wooden shaft between wheel horses, connected to front axle; tongue.

pole strap. Connection between horses' collars and foremost end of pole and swing pole; breast strap.

reach. Shaft connecting fore and hind gear of coach; perch.

sorrel. Brown, red-yellow in hue. Horses are often identified by their color: bay, dull reddish-brown; brindle, grey streaked or spotted with dark; roan, reddish-brown mixed with grey or white; buckskin, tannish-brown.

stage. Portion of route between relay points or stations.

stand. Secondary relay point between stations for occasional use.

swing pole. Wooden pole between swing horses.

swing station. Relay point along route where teams were changed.

swing team. Team of horses between lead and wheel teams.

wainwright. Builder of wagons.

wheel team. Team nearest wheels.

ACKNOWLEDGMENTS

The author is deeply indebted to Mr. George Rouff, Placerville, California; Mr. Edward Tierney, Rawlins, Wyoming; Mr. Burt Acree, Austin, Nevada; Mr. Earl Matthews, Concord, New Hampshire; Mr. Carroll D. Hall, Supervisor, Fr. Sutter Museum, Sacramento, California; to the Placerville, California, Chamber of Commerce; the Society of California Pioneers; the Wells Fargo Bank; the New Hampshire Historical Society, and many others for their help and friendship.

The author is pleased to acknowledge the following sources for actual photographs, drawings, etc. used in this book.

"Overland Mail Coach Crossing Rocky Mountains, 1868" *Harper's Weekly,* Feb. 8, 1868. Courtesy Bancroft Library, University of California, Berkeley, California.

Mail Coach from Abbott, Downing and Company Catalogue.

Stage Harness from J. R. Hill and Company Catalogue. Courtesy Sutter's Fort Museum, Sacramento, California.

Clipper Ship from *American Neptune,* Pictorial Supplement 1, 1959.

Mud Wagon drawing. Courtesy Sutter's Fort Museum.

Drawings of Concord Mail Coach from *American Horse-Drawn Vehicles.* Courtesy J. D. Rittenhouse.

Photograph of Concord Mail Coach. Courtesy Union Pacific Railroad.

Hame and Concord Harness. Courtesy Sutter's Fort Museum.

Newspaper ad. Courtesy Denver Public Library, Western History Department.

Spencer Rifle. Courtesy Society of California Pioneers.

Henry Rifle. Courtesy Olin Mathieson Chemical Corporation.

Indian Drawing. Courtesy Smithsonian Institution, B.A.E. #1471-a-1.

California Stage Company Advertisement from *1856-57 San Francisco City Directory.* Courtesy Bancroft Library, University of California.

Painting of Central Overland and Pike's Peak Express Coach. Courtesy St. Joseph Public Library.

Photograph of Locomotive. Courtesy Union Pacific Railroad.

BIBLIOGRAPHY

The following books and magazines were valuable sources of information in the preparation of *Overland Stage:*

Banning, William, and Banning, G. H. *Six Horses.* New York: Appleton-Century Co., Inc., 1930.

Clemens, Samuel Langhorne (Mark Twain) *Roughing It.* New York: Harper and Brothers, 1875.

The September, 1939 issue of *The Colorado Magazine.*

Hafen, LeRoy R. *Overland Mail 1849-1869.* Limited ed. Cleveland: Arthur H. Clark Co., 1926.

The November, 1945 issue of *Historical New Hampshire.*

Root, F. A., and Connelley, William E. *Overland Stage to California.* Columbus: Long's College Book Co., 1901.

FRONTIER WEST BOOKS

Overland Stage

The story of the famous Overland Stagecoaches of the 1860's
Written and illustrated by Glen Dines

Long Knife

The story of the fighting U. S. Cavalry of the 1860 frontier
Written and illustrated by Glen Dines

Silver and Lead

The birth and death of a mining town
Written by Ralph Moody
Illustrated by Charles W. Walker

Buffalo Land

The untamed wilderness of the high plains frontier
Written and illustrated by William D. Berry

Dog Soldiers

The famous warrior society of the Cheyenne Indians
Written by Glen Dines and Raymond Price
Illustrated by Peter Burchard